Featherstrokes For Shorebirds

Beebe Hopper

West Chester, Pennsylvania 19380

Beebe Hopper is the author of several wildfowl publications which can be purchased at your local art and craft supply store, bookstore or write to:

Beebe Hopper
731 Beech Avenue
Chula Vista, CA 92010

"Featherstrokes, The Basics of Painting Feathers"
"Featherstrokes for Canvasbacks"
"Featherstrokes for Mallards"
"Wildfowl Painting"
"Painting Wild Geese"

Completed shorebirds in this book have been hand carved by Jim Hopper.
Photography by Michael Armbrust, Chula Vista, CA.
Study skins courtesy of the San Diego Museum of Natural History.
Shorebird blanks may be obtained from several different manufacturers including Big Sky Carvers, Bozeman, MT and Dolington Woodcrafts, Newtown, PA.
If needed painting supplies are not available through your local art supply store, write to Beebe Hopper at the above address.

Published by Schiffer Publishing, Ltd.
1469 Morstein Road
West Chester, Pennsylania 19380
Please write for a free catalog
This book may be purchased from the publisher.
Please include $2.00 postage.
Try your bookstore first.

Printed in the United States of America.
ISBN: 0-88740-176-7

Contents

DEDICATION

To my husband, Jim, who has supported,
suggested, given constructive criticism and
been with me all the way.

Introduction

There is an easy way to paint realistic feathers for wildfowl painting! That is what the "featherstroke technique" is all about. The presentation is so simple that anyone who can hold a paint brush can quickly master rendering realistic feathers. A feather is a feather is a feather, whether it is on a duck, goose, songbird, shorebird, hummingbird, chicken, bird-of-paradise or whatever the species of fowl may be. The feather painting techniques taught in this book are just one approach. They are simple, easy methods which provide the beginner with the background for successful painting from the start. The featherstroke techniques can be used on textured carvings, carvings with the feather pattern burned in, or on smooth surfaces. The techniques can also be used on canvas or other media surfaces, with oils, acrylics, or watercolor. The only difference will occur in the consistency of the paint. Acrylics are the simplest media for the beginner learning these methods. Acrylics hold the bristles of the brush in the desired positions for different shapes and sizes of feather effects. You must work harder at learning and achieving the right consistency for the oil or watercolor medias. As you experiment and practice mixing and painting with various media, you will develop a "feel" for the paint on the brush and be able to achieve the proper consistency.

Do not be afraid to begin! Remember, it is not yet a great work of art, it is only a piece of wood, canvas or paper! You can repaint it as many times as you choose. Putting this thought into perspective gives you the psychological freedom to begin to create. So why are you waiting?

Supplies

Supplies used throughout this book are listed below.

Acrylic Matte Medium—Used as a protective or finish coat on completed wildfowl carvings.

Palette—The wax coated, disposable palette is very convenient. A piece of glass with white cardboard or paper underneath provides a firm surface for fanning the Kats Tongue brush.

Paper Towels—Several folded thicknesses of paper towels will be needed for blotting of excess water and paint from your brush.

Painting Knife—A flat blade knife can be used to mix your colors. Personally, I prefer to mix color with a brush. I feel that by mixing the color with a brush, one achieves more depth and vibrancy.

Fine Grade Sandpaper—For smoothing rough areas of waterfowl.

Water Container—A brush basin, plastic bowl or glass jar for washing your brushes.

Exacto Knife—To clean the paint off the eyes of finished carvings.

Pencil—HB or 2B for sketching and drawing on surfaces.

Acrylic Colors—The brand of paint that I prefer to use is Permalba for several reasons. It is a professional quality paint with high intensity of color; the shelf life is long; and most importantly, the basic and iridescent colors used in painting wildfowl have been formulated to exactly match the color of the different feathers.

Titanium White—A pure white, used alone for highlights or mixed with colors to create tints and hues.

Unbleached Titanium—An off-white used with almost any color, especially Raw Umber to create the many shades needed to paint feathers.

Raw Umber—A dark, grayish-brown which is the most important color in painting most birds. Please note, there is a vast difference in the Raw Umber made by different manufacturers of artists' colors. Permalba Raw Umber has been formulated to properly match the color native to so many birds, whether it is used as a single coat or as a layered wash of color.

Black—Ivory or Mars. Ivory Black is warmer and more transparent than other blacks. Mars Black is a rich opaque. It is a color used to shade other hues for the application of the darks.

Burnt Umber—A rich, dark, warm earth tone brown used throughout wildfowl painting.

Burnt Sienna—A reddish brown, very warm

earth tone applied throughout the painting process.

Cadmium Orange—A bright mid-value orange used in mixtures for color areas such as the bills of wildfowl.

Cadmium Red Light—A bright orange-red color.

Cadmium Red Medium—A rich, intense red mixed with other hues to create some of the bright areas of certain species.

Cadmium Yellow Medium—A rich, bright, middle-value yellow for application in color mixtures. A color not typically used alone in wildfowl painting.

Hookers Green—A dark, transparent forest green used in certain wildfowl species.

Paynes Gray—A cool, steel gray applied in the body and bill sections of many of the wildfowl species.

Phthalo Blue—A middle value blue, vibrant, toward the greenish hue.

Phthalo Green—A middle value green toward the bluish hue.

Ultramarine Blue—An intense, bright blue used in the speculum of some wildfowl species.

Yellow Ochre—A light, natural earth tone used throughout wildfowl painting.

Iridescent Gold—A sparkling, dazzling gold used in feather painting and color mixtures.

Iridescent Green—a deep green with sparking effects used in some head and speculum areas of wildfowl species.

Iridescent Blue—A dazzling blue for application in speculum and other iridescent areas of some wildfowl species.

Iridescent Purple—A deep purple with a rainbow-like glow used in select areas of wildfowl painting.

Iridescent Crimson—A vibrant, dazzling red used in mixing of other colors to attain different hues for feathers.

Iridescent White—A pure white hue with a sparkling glitter-like effect which can be added to a standard color to give iridescence.

Materials

Important! Good tools work for you, inferior tools work against you. So please, have the very best brushes, paints, carving blanks, canvas and paper available. The materials that you use are your tools, and the quality of your work is in direct relationship to the quality of these tools.

Media—For "painting in the round" (carving and sculpting), I prefer to use acrylics. Fast drying is the prime advantage of acrylics. It enables you to finish an item without long delays. Drying time is much longer when working with oils. The use of a hair dryer speeds the drying process of acrylics immeasurably. Blending of acrylic colors, however, is a problem for many. A special hint for this is to keep the working areas damp, thus enabling the colors to flow and blend together with ease.

Brushes—The value of good quality brushes cannot be stressed enough. The Beebe Hopper Feather Painting Brushes are manufactured by Langnickel, Inc. who for 50 years has made brushes of the finest quality. The Kats Tongue has been a mainstay for me in oils and in painting dimensional carved wildfowl. The brush adapts beautifully to realistic feather painting. The Shader is ideal for canvas painting, especially laying in backgrounds.

When this brush is used as a shader for wildfowl feather painting, the results, without a doubt, are unmatchable. The Liner works well with all media. The bristles are long enough to give the freedom of a rigger brush, but short enough for control of detail work.

There are three basic elements to each brush: the hair, the metal ferrule and the wooden handle. The hair selected for the head of the brush, animal or synthetic, is the most important element. It must have resiliency, durability and the quality to keep a point or hold a sharp edge.

Brush hair falls into two categories: soft and stiff. Stiff bristles are usually hog or nylon. Soft hairs generally used are kolinsky, weasel, ox, sabeline, squirrel, pony and goat. The "red sable", as it is known to artists, comes from different species of the squirrel, weasel or rodent family which live in cold climates, not from the sable animal. Various raw materials for brushes are listed below with a short description of each. Please familiarize yourself with these different types to enable you to distinguish the quality levels of brushes when purchasing them.

Kolinsky—Known as "Finest Red Sable", this hair, possessing exceptional spring and fine pointing quality, comes from the kolinsky, the largest of the Red Tartar Marten species which is native to northern China, southern Russia and Siberia. Only the hairs from the tail are used.

Weasel—Known as Fine or Good Quality red sable, these hairs come from the tails of the Weasel family.

Squirrel—A very soft hair taken from tails of different species of squirrel. Painting quality is excellent.

Goat—A soft hair used in lesser quality and cosmetic brushes.

Pony—From the mane and body of ponies.

Hog—The bristles of the spinal section of wild boars from northern China are used for the top of the line white bristle brushes.

Nylon—A man-made synthetic product used alone or blended with various natural hairs for all styles of brushes. Quality varies a great deal. Until recently, synthetic brushes were not produced at a very high quality level. Today there are some high quality synthetic brushes being produced.

Ox—Taken from oxen native to central Europe and North and South America.

Sabeline—A medium grade hair used for watercolor, lettering and stroke work. These are made from dyed ox hair.

Handles—The wooden handles are made from hardwood in either long or short lengths. Wooden handles are usually coated with a sturdy laquer paint. Plastic handles are generally used with synthetic bristles.

Ferrules—Nickel plated brass or aluminum is used. Most ferrules are seamless to prevent splitting.

Techniques and Basics

Preparation—To paint a dimensional wildfowl decoy, you must start with a well-sanded and primed bird. First, apply a wood sealer to the entire carving. Let dry. After the carving is sealed, apply a white base primer coat. This can be acrylic, latex paint or a gesso product. After the prime coat has dried, sand smooth with a fine grade sandpaper.

Featherstroking—The Featherstroke technique with the Kats Tongue brush is simple and ideal to use for painting the individual feathers of the different species. A large sized Kats Tongue brush will create very small feathers. On the other hand, a small sized brush will not make feathers larger than when it is fanned to its maximum width. The Kats Tongue #12 is used almost exclusively. One exception is for large-sized carvings such as geese or diving duck hens. A Kats Tongue #18 is used for these birds. The Kats Tongue brush will need to be "trained" to hold the proper form for featherstroking. To "train" this brush, remember to use it in the same direction each time that you paint. This is easy to remember if you use it with the writing on the handle facing away from you.

Work the brush into the paint and water thoroughly. Fan the brush by pressing down firmly all the way to the ferrule. Twist carefully back and forth and the brush will form a fan shape. Refer to Photo #1. Slowly draw the brush backward and upward in the same motion. This is an important stroke motion to learn. Refer to Photo #2. This

Photo #1.

Photo #2.

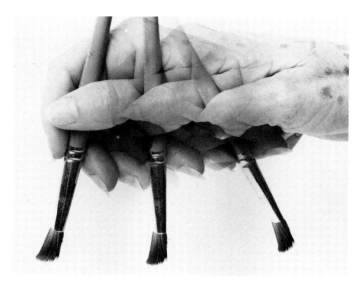

Photo #3.

Photo #4.

Illustration #1.

Illustration #2.

Photo #5.

action will form an arc of the bristles. The brush is now ready to paint featherstrokes. You must remember that a light touch, using thin paint, is necessary when painting feathers. To paint feathers, hold the brush almost upright, and using a flick of the fingers, lightly stroke the bristles toward yourself. Refer to Photo #3 and Illustration #1. For creating a smaller sized feather, reduce the arc of the fan by rolling the sides of the brush inward. Refer to Photo #4 and Illustration #2. For smaller feathers, reduce the arc again. Refer to Photo #5 and Illustration #3. To paint tiny feathers for the head and neck areas of birds, press the sides of the arc together with your fingers to form a "tent" or inverted "V". Refer to Photo #6 and Illustration #4. Hold the brush perpendicular to the surface, and with a

Illustration #3.

Photo #6.

Illustration #4.

Photo #7.

Photo #8.

Photo #9.

light touch, paint the tiny feathers. If bristles split or separate, use more paint, but only enough to hold the bristles in the desired position. The angle of the brush when drawing it back and up off the palette determines the deepness or shallowness of the arc for the featherstroke. When the brush handle is at a high angle during this action, the featherstroke arc is deeper. Refer to Photo #7. When the handle is at a lower angle, the arc for the featherstroke is shallower. Refer to Photo #8.

Linework—The Liner brush is used for fine line detail painting and also makes great grass and twiggy trees in landscape painting. To complete the linework technique, the paint should be the consistency of ink. Saturate the brush with thin paint, when lifting the brush off the palette, roll the brush to form a sharp point. Brace your hand and use only the tip of the brush. Refer to Photo #9 and Illustration #5. This brush works like a fountain pen. When the brush is saturated with thin paint, as you stroke, the paint flows down to the tip.

Shading—The Shader brush is ideal for canvas painting, especially for applying foundations in backgrounds. The bristles come to a fine razor edge and are used for shading the elongated feathers of birds. Refer to Photo #10 and Illustration #6.

13

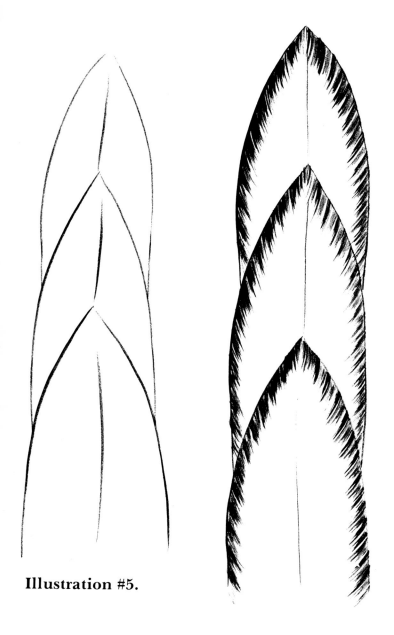

Illustration #5.

Illustration #6.

Illustration #7.

Photo #10.

Washes—A wash simply means a small amount of paint mixed into a larger amount of water. There are thin washes, medium washes and heavy washes. It is difficult to define exact amounts. A "rule of thumb" for a thin wash is one drop of paint to thirty drops of water; for a medium wash, the procedure would be more paint into the water; and, for a heavy wash, even more paint mixed into the water. Refer to Illustration #7.

Finishing—One way to finish a carving is by applying a generous coat of acrylic Matte Medium over the completed bird. This gives a satin finish, neither dull nor glossy. The acrylic Matte Medium looks very milky upon application, but when dry becomes transparent. Apply the acrylic Matte Medium in a very even application with a soft hair varnish or sponge brush.

Tips

1. Always keep your brushes clean!! Wash them thoroughly with soap and water to remove all color, paying careful attention to the area near the metal ferrule. Rinse the brush thoroughly and shape it with your fingers to form the natural shape. Never let a brush dry when bristles are separated.

2. *MOTH PROOF YOUR BRUSHES!!* Moths love good, natural hair brushes, especially red sable. When you do not use your brushes often, please store them in a moth proof area.

3. When using acrylics, a drop or two of detergent added to the painting water helps to remove pigment when changing from one color to another.

4. Each coat of acrylic must be thoroughly dry before applying the next coat, whether it is a wash or a regular coat of paint. If not, the wet coat underneath will come off and you will have an area to repair that takes both time and effort.

5. Acrylics will not hurt your red sable brush, *if you keep your brushes clean!* Dried acrylic paint in brushes is very difficult to remove. There are several products on the market which will soften acrylic that has hardened in the brush. Check with your local art and craft shop for these products. Rubbing alcohol will soften acrylic. What-ever the product used, it will take time and effort to reclaim your brushes. But you can do it; persistence pays dividends.

6. REMEMBER! The end of the feather always points toward the tail of the bird, otherwise the feather will appear to be growing backward on the bird.

7. Painting strokes should follow the contour of the bird. The contour directions of the feathers of birds are depicted in Illustration #8 A and B.

8. Feathers should connect, both front and back and side to side. No open "rows" of feathers should occur.

Illustration #8A.

15

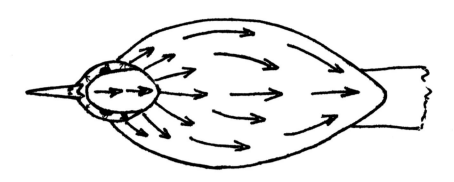

Illustration #8 B.

9. Collect reference material. Begin a library of bird books or any subject in which you are interested. Pictures from magazines and papers are good sources from which to collect.

10. Never let a brush dry when bristles are split or separated. Wet the brush and with your fingers, form it into it's natural shape.

IMPORTANT! The painting techniques used in this book are as easily applied to canvas as they are to "in the round" pieces. The stroke action and paint application is the same.

Prime Coat—A prime coat of white paint is desirable. The white will reflect the colors applied over it, thus giving more life to the colors used. Frequently, I use acrylic Titanium White as a primer. Permalba gesso is so finely ground that little sanding is required. Other materials used are latex house paint and flat spray paint.

READ COMPLETE INSTRUCTIONS BEFORE BEGINNING TO PAINT!!

An abstract color pattern is given with each species instruction. Paint the full base color on each bird before beginning the finishing techniques.

REMEMBER!! Think thin and soft. Soft strokes, thin paint!

Bases

The base on which you display your carving should be carefully selected for the overall aesthetic value of the piece.

The ways of display are as many and varied as there are carvers and carvings. The following are brief comments on some of the most popular methods of display. There are custom made bases designed for a particular work, bases of natural wood; i.e., driftwood. There are roots, limbs, shells, cork floats, etc.

The history of some are very interesting. Around the turn of the century, there were many sawmills along the shores of Lake Michigan. These mills dumped the scrap lumber into the lake at depths up to 60 feet. The sand, silt and water action have polished the "knots" of this cast-off lumber to a driftwood like finish. Highwood Bookshop,

Traverse City, MI employs a diver to gather these knots from this deep water; they make interesting and appropriate bases.

Birds of a Feather, New Britain, CT manufactures router-milled bases of many varieties of wood, styles and finishes. They will manufacture bases to your specifications.

John and Orchid Davis of A Change of Scene, Westminster, SC carry in stock natural wood bases of manzanita roots and driftwood.

Wildlife Arts and Crafts Manufacturing Company, Salisbury, MD always has a large selection of natural driftwood. There are many other sources throughout the country of which I am not aware. Whatever base you choose for your carving, it should compliment the piece in design and texture.

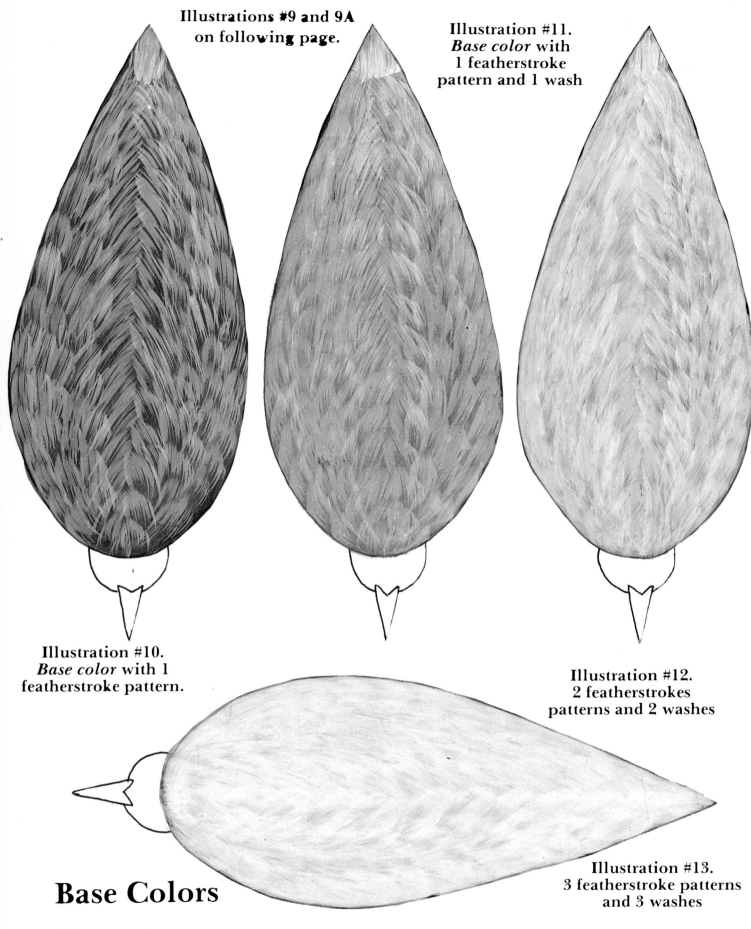

Illustrations #9 and 9A
on following page.

Illustration #11.
Base color with
1 featherstroke
pattern and 1 wash

Illustration #10.
Base color with 1
featherstroke pattern.

Illustration #12.
2 featherstrokes
patterns and 2 washes

Illustration #13.
3 featherstroke patterns
and 3 washes

Base Colors

Illustration #9. Underbody Colors
Raw Umber + Yellow Ochre = *Base Color*

Illustration #14.
Base color with
one shading of
unbleached Titanium

Illustration #15.
Plus 1 wash of
Raw Umber

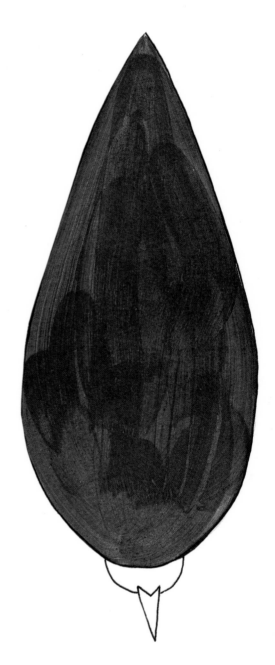

Illustration #16.
2 shadings
and 2 washes

Illustration #17.

Illustration #9A.
Base color underbody

19

Projects

Killdeer

Killdeer are the best known of the plover family. They inhabit all parts of our nation from shore to grasslands and farmlands, to city parks and open spaces of the interior. Identification is easy by voice ("kill-dee, kill-dee") and by sight. They have two black breast bands and an orange-brown rump making identification simple.

As with other species of shorebirds, killdeer are very protective of their nest and young. When danger threatens, they will effect a "broken wing" action, fluttering along the ground away from the nest area to distract the intruder. Frequently, they follow closely to farmers who are plowing their fields, gathering from the freshly turned earth the insects that form a large portion of their diet.

Killdeer are indeed handsome birds; bird-lovers have long enjoyed their song and behavior.

Colors—Titanium White, Black, Raw Umber, Unbleached Titanium, Burnt Umber, Yellow Ochre, Orange, Burnt Sienna, and Cadmium Red Light.
Brushes—Liner #0, Shader #10, Kats Tongue #8 or 12; soft, round #10.

Prior to painting the carving, sand the blank smooth. Apply a wood sealer to the entire blank and let dry. When sealer is dry, apply a prime coat of white paint, refer to section on primers, page 16. When dry, lightly sand to create a smooth surface. Draw in abstract areas and apply base colors as indicated. Refer to Illustration #18 and 18A as a guide. Use Liner #0 with black paint the consistency of ink.

Illustration #18.
Base Colors

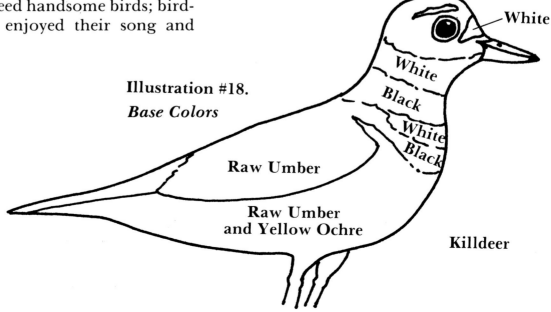

Killdeer

Killdeer Illustration #19.

Killdeer Illustration #20.

Illustration #18A.
Base Colors

Killdeer

Photo #12.

Photo #13.

Photo #14.

Photo #15.

Killdeer

Photo #16.

Back, Head and Neck—(White and black areas will be overpainted later.) Draw in feather pattern on back using Liner #0 and black paint. Refer to Illustration #19 and 20 as a guide. Head and shoulder feathers are painted with Unbleached Titanium using Kats Tongue #8 or 12. Refer to Photo #2 and 3 and Illustration #2 and 3. Create the feather pattern by stroking color on from the edge of the feather inward. To paint the elongated feathers, use Shader #10, shading from outside edge inward with Unbleached Titanium. Refer to Illustration #14, 15 and 16. When pattern is complete, apply a thin wash of Raw Umber. Repeat feather application and washes until desired softness is achieved.

Tail and Lower Back Rump—Orange-Red. Mix a small amount of Burnt Umber into Orange with a touch of Red. Apply this mix to base area of tail and blend into black towards the end. Bottom edges are shaded in white.

Underbody—Refer to Illustration 9 and 9A. Using a soft, round size 10, fan the brush until it has a "ragged" appearance. With Unbleached Titanium and beginning at the tail, make short, sweeping featherstrokes (no more than 1/2" long) slightly angled inward at the center. Apply these strokes to the whole of the underside. Refer to Illustration #10. Apply a wash of Titanium White mixed with a *very small amount* of Unbleached Titanium. The Unbleached Titanium will prohibit a chalky look to the white. Refer to Illustration #11.

Repeat feather pattern and wash. Refer to Illustration #12.

Repeat feather pattern and wash. Refer to Illustration #13.

This method of paint and wash application will achieve a soft, feathery appearance.

The whole chest will be feathered white, black chest rings will be overpainted. Paint the chest ring on breast and belly.

Primaries—Brownish-Black. Mix together Raw Umber with a small amount of Black as a base color. With medium gray, draw in feather pattern using Liner #0. Stroke from outer edge inward using Shader #10 with Unbleached Titanium (thin). Apply a thin black wash to soften. Refer to Photo #16.

Bill—Black

Eye Ring—Red

Legs and Feet—Grayish-yellow. Paint in white areas on neck and head. Paint in black chest rings, blending into the adjacent colors to give a feathered look.

Sanderling

This little shorebird evokes more emotion in people than any other. It is the one we see along the shoreline scurrying back and forth as the waves come ashore. Seldom do we ever see one caught by incoming surf. These romantic little gray and white birds are found on all of our coastlines. They prefer sandy beaches to probe for the small mollusks, flies and worms which make up most of their diet. The gray back and white underbelly are the winter plumage, and the more colorful breeding plumage is usually seen only in their breeding grounds in the arctic region.

Colors—Titanium White, Black, Unbleached Titanium, Raw Umber, Yellow Ochre

Brushes—Liner #0, Shader #10, Kats Tongue #12, soft, round #10. Before beginning to paint the carved blank, you should lightly sand the blank to be sure it is smooth. Apply a wood sealer to the entire blank and let dry. When dry, apply a prime coat of paint. Refer to section on primers, page 16.

Draw in abstract areas and paint base colors as indicated. Refer to Illustration #21 and 21A.

Underbody and Face—Refer to Illustrations #9 and 9A. The base color is equal parts of Raw Umber and Yellow Ochre. Refer to

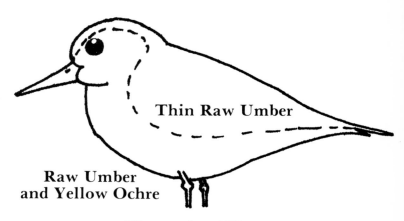

Thin Raw Umber

Raw Umber and Yellow Ochre

Illustration #21.

Illustration #21A. Using a soft, round brush size 10, fan the brush until it has a "ragged" appearance. With White and a touch of Unbleached Titanium, begin at the tail, make short sweeping featherstrokes (no more than 1/2" long), slightly angled inward at the center. Apply these strokes to the whole of the underside. Refer to Illustration #10. Apply a wash of Titanium White mixed with a very small amount of Unbleached Titanium. The Unbleached Titanium will prohibit a chalky look to the white. Refer to Illustration #11.

Repeat feather pattern and wash. Refer to Illustration #12.

Repeat feather pattern and wash. Refer to Illustration #13.

Thin Raw Umber

Sanderling

Illustration #21A.

**Raw Umber
and Yellow Ochre**

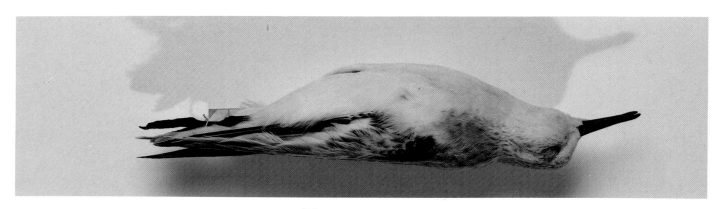

Photo #17.

Photo #18.

Photo #19.

Photo #20.

Sanderling

Photo #21.

Sanderling Illustration #22.

This method of paint and wash application will achieve a soft, feathery appearance.

Top of Head and Back—Draw in feather pattern on back using Liner #0. Refer to Illustration #22 and 23 as a guide. For the rounded head and shoulder feathers, reduce the Kats Tongue #12, refer to photos #4, 5, and 6 OR use Kats Tongue #8. To paint the elongated feathers, use Shader #10. Refer to Illustrations #14 thru #16. Paint feather pattern over entire back section using Unbleached Titanium, refer to photos #2 and 3, Illustration #3 for instructions for feathering. When pattern is complete, apply a thin wash of mixture of Raw Umber and a *touch* of black. Repeat feather application over same areas and apply a second wash of the gray mix. Continue this process until desired softness of feathers is achieved.

Primaries—Draw in feather outline using Liner #0 with Black. Stroke from outer edge inward using the Shader #10 with thin Unbleached Titanium. Refer to Illustration #14 thru 16. Apply a thin wash of Raw Umber to soften. Paint last primary black and shade with dark gray.

Legs, Feet and Bill—Black

Eye Detail—White ring around eye. Use Liner #0 for black detail markings.

Sanderling Illustration #23.

28

Ruddy Turnstone

Ruddy Turnstones in breeding plumage are beautiful birds. They are one of a very few species of shorebirds which use their bill as a tool. The name Ruddy Turnstone is very appropriate because parts of feathers in spring plumage turn into a bright cinnamon or ruddy color. The bill is used to flip and overturn stones and shells seeking the small crustaceans and shorelife underneath. They have bright orange-red legs and feet.

It is indeed fascinating to watch a group of turnstones "work" a rocky shoreline searching for food.

Colors—Titanium White, Black, Burnt Sienna, Yellow Ochre, Raw Umber

Brushes—Liner #0, Shader #10, soft, round #10, Kats Tongue #12.

The carved bird should be well-sanded to ensure smoothness. Apply a wood sealer to whole bird blank and let dry. Apply a prime coat of paint, let dry and resand. Refer to section on primers, page 16. Draw in abstract areas and paint base colors indicated, blending each color into the other. Refer to Illustration #24 and 24A.

Underbody—Refer to Illustrations #9 and 9A. Using a soft, round brush, size 10, fan the brush until it has a "ragged appearance.

With Unbleached Titanium and beginning at the tail, make short sweeping feather-strokes (no more than 1/2" long) slightly angled inward at the center. Apply these strokes to the whole underside. Refer to Illustration #10. Apply a wash of Titanium White mixed with a very small amount of Unbleached Titanium. The Unbleached Titanium will prohibit a chalky look to the white. Refer to Illustration #11.

Repeat feather pattern and wash. Refer to Illustration #12.

Repeat feather pattern and wash. Refer to Illustration #13.

This method of paint and wash application will achieve a soft, feathery appearance.

The whole underbody will be feathered white; black areas will be overpainted.

Head and Neck—Paint with white. To detail head, use Liner #0, making uneven black markings down crown. Edge with Yellow Ochre.

Back—Base coat in light Burnt Sienna. Draw in feather pattern on back with Black using Liner #0. Refer to Illustration #25 and 26 as a guide. Paint black feather areas. Highlight the outer edge of the black feathers with gray (black and white) using Shader #10. Stroke from outer edge inward. If harsh, apply a thin black wash. Highlight the

Illustration #24A.

Ruddy Turnstone

Photo #22.

Photo #23.

Photo #24.

Photo #25.

Ruddy Turnstone

Photo #26.

russet feathers with a mixture of Unbleached Titanium and Burnt Sienna. To soften, apply a light wash of Burnt Sienna. Continue the feathering and wash steps until desired softness is achieved. Refer to Photo #26.

Primaries—Draw in feather outline using Liner #0 and Black. Highlight the outer edge with Shader #10 and using the Unbleached Titanium. Stroke from the outer edge in. To soften, apply a thin Burnt Sienna wash.

Paint the last primary black and shade with dark gray. Refer to Photo #26.

Shoulders and Chest—Paint with black and blend into all areas to create a softened line. Use Kats Tongue #12 to feather with dark gray paint. Refer to Illustrations #3 and 4.

Bill—Black
Legs and Feet—Dark Red
Tail—black shaded in dark gray

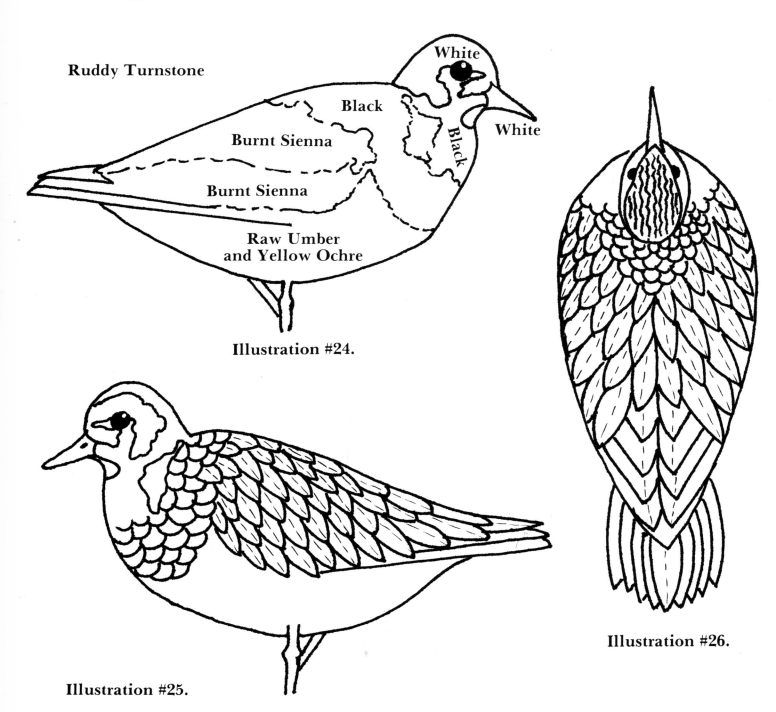

Ruddy Turnstone

White

Black

White

Black

Black

Burnt Sienna

Burnt Sienna

Raw Umber and Yellow Ochre

Illustration #24.

Illustration #25.

Illustration #26.

Long Billed Curlew

The Long Billed Curlew is the largest of the North American shorebirds. This stately bird inhabits grasslands of the midwest with his territory extending to the mudflats of the Gulf and Pacific coasts. Infrequently, one may be seen along the Atlantic Coast. The bill is very long and decurved. They feed in the estuarian mud flats by probing the full length of this great bill into the soft mud for mud shrimp and crustaceans. In the grasslands, the diet varies more widely to include worms, insects, berries, etc.

A few years ago it was a great thrill for me to see a flock of several dozen of these magnificent buff and cinnamon colored birds in the San Joaquin Valley of California apparently as they were migrating northward. Each year we see what appears to be the same bird upon its return to the mudflats of south San Diego Bay. He is usually alone and once in a while a second, smaller bird will appear. Other parts of the bay have a number of curlews.

Colors—Titanium White, Black, Raw Umber, Unbleached Titanium, Cadmium Red Medium, Burnt Sienna, Yellow Ochre

Brushes—Liner #0, Shader #10, Kats Tongue #12, soft, round #10. Before beginning to paint, sand the carved blank to ensure that it is smooth. Apply a wood sealer to the entire blank and let dry. Apply a prime coat of paint, when dry lightly resand. See section on primers, page 16.

Draw in abstract areas and paint base colors indicated. Refer to Illustrations #27 and 27A.

Underbody—Refer to Illustrations #9 and 9A. Using a soft, round size 10, fan the brush until it has a "ragged" appearance. With Unbleached Titanium and beginning at the tail, make short sweeping featherstrokes (no more than 1/2" long) slightly angled inward at the center. Apply these strokes to the whole underbody. Refer to Illustration #10.

Apply a wash using Unbleached Titanium with a touch of Burnt Sienna, a light cinnamon color. Refer to Illustration #11 for technique.

Repeat feather pattern and wash. Refer to Illustration #12.

Repeat feather pattern and wash. Refer to Illustration #13.

This method of paint and wash application will achieve a soft, feathery appearance.

Back, Head and Back of Neck—Draw in feather pattern on back and shoulders referring to Illustration #28 and 29 as a guide. Shade in edges of elongated feathers using Shader #10 and Unbleached Titanium.

**Long Billed Curlew
Illustration #27A.**
Base Colors

Thin Raw Umber

Raw Umber and Yellow Ochre

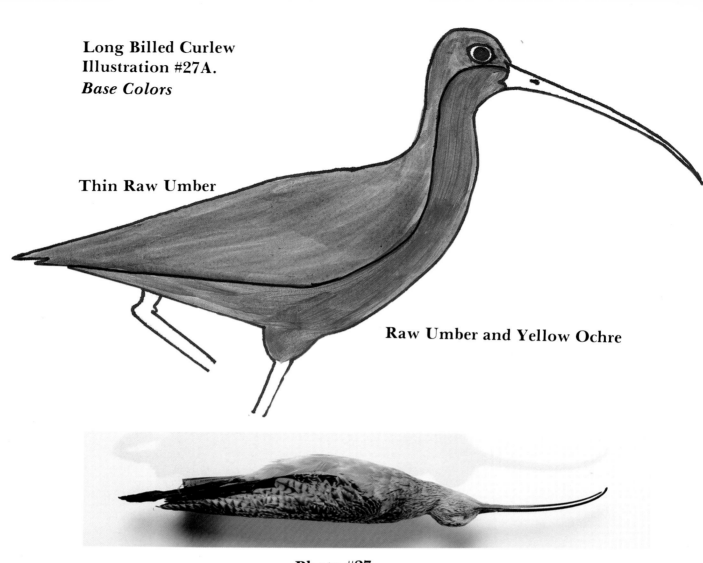

Photo #27.

Photo #28.

Photo #29.

Photo #30.

Long Billed Curlew

Photo #31.

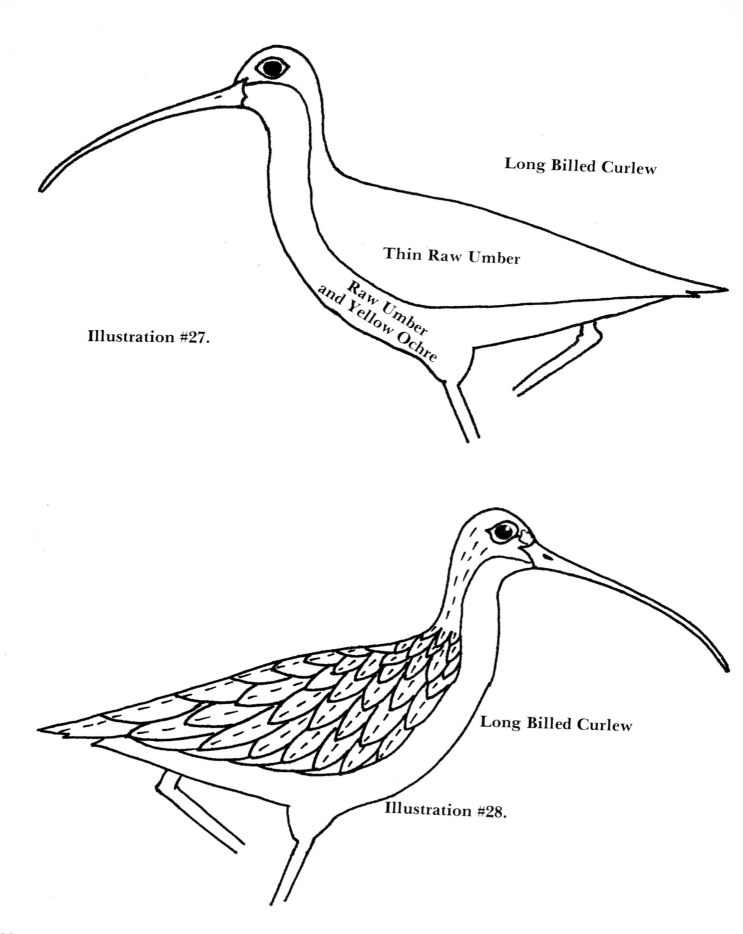

Long Billed Curlew

Thin Raw Umber

Raw Umber
and Yellow Ochre

Illustration #27.

Long Billed Curlew

Illustration #28.

Refer to Illustration #14. Apply a wash of Raw Umber. Refer to Illustration #15. Repeat above step. Refer to Illustration #16. Head and neck are feathered with Kats Tongue #8, refer to Photo #4, 5, and 6. Apply a wash of thin Raw Umber. Repeat shading and wash procedures until desired softness is achieved. When desired softness is achieved, finish elongated feathers and barred side feathers using Liner #0 with Black to make the "swept wing" design in each feather. Refer to Illustration #17 and Photo #31.

Head and Neck Detail—Using Liner #0, paint thin, short strokes with Raw Umber over crown and down back of neck with a lesser amount of strokes in front and down to chest area. Underchin is white, a white area at side top of bill and a white ring around the eye.

Legs—Gray

Bill—Lower mandible is flesh color; upper is black. Mix Cadmium Red Medium, Unbleached Titanium with a touch of Raw Umber.

Long Billed Curlew
Illustration #29.

Spotted Sandpiper

Illustration #30A.
Base Colors

Photo #32.

Photo #33.

Photo #34.

Spotted Sandpiper

Photo #35.

The Spotted Sandpiper is one of the most interesting of the many species of sandpipers. As it searches for food, it moves with a "bobbing" motion of the rear half of its body. They have short legs and in breeding plumage have distinctive black spots on the white underparts. This species inhabits almost all parts of North America from salt water estuaries to high mountain timberline. Many times while fishing Montana streams, I've watched their "bobbing" gait as they search for food along the muddy banks. This always makes the fishing worthwhile, even if the fish don't bite.

Colors—Titanium White, Black, Raw Umber, Unbleached Titanium, Burnt Sienna, Yellow Ochre.

Brushes—Liner #0, Shader #10, Kats Tongue #12, soft, flat #2 and soft, round #10.

Before beginning to paint, sand the carved blank to ensure that it is smooth. Apply a wood sealer to the entire blank and let dry. Apply a prime coat of paint, when dry lightly resand. See section on primers, page 16.

Draw in abstract areas and paint base colors as indicated. Refer to Illustration #30 and 30A.

Underbody—Refer to Illustrations #9 and 9A. Using a soft, round brush size 10, fan the brush until it has a "ragged" appearance. With Unbleached Titanium and beginning at the tail, make short sweeping feather-strokes (no more than 1/2" long) slightly angled inward at the center. Apply these strokes to the whole underside. Refer to Illustration #10.

Apply a wash of Titanium White mixed with a very small amount of Unbleached Titanium. The Unbleached Titanium will prohibit a chalky look to the white. Refer to Illustration #11.

Repeat feather pattern and wash. Refer to Illustration #12.

Repeat feather pattern and wash. Refer to Illustration #13.

Paint in black spots over belly area with Black and using a soft, flat #2 brush.

Top of Head and Back—Draw in feather pattern on back referring to Illustration #31 and 32 as a guide, using Liner #0 with black paint. For the rounded feathers of the head and shoulders, use Kats Tongue #8 OR reduce Kats Tongue #12. Refer to Photos 4, 5 and 6. To paint the elongated feathers, use Shader #10 with Unbleached Titanium and stroking from outside edge inward to form

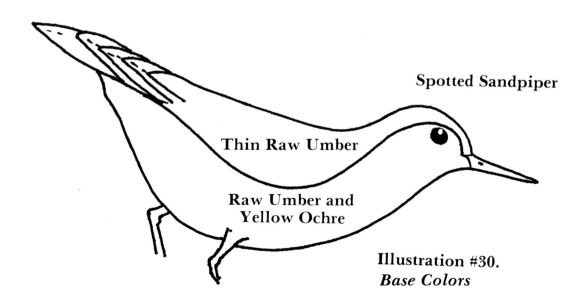

Spotted Sandpiper

Thin Raw Umber

Raw Umber and Yellow Ochre

Illustration #30.
Base Colors

40

highlight. Refer to Illustration #14, 15 and 16. Apply a thin wash of Raw Umber. Repeat procedure until desired softness is achieved. Using Liner #0 with Black, paint bars on long feathers and small "swept wing" design on rounded feathers of back and shoulders. Refer to Illustration #17 and Photo #35.

Primaries—Base coat the primary feathers in Black. Draw in feather outline using Liner #0. Shade from outer edge inward with a dark gray mixture of Black with a touch of Unbleached Titanium.

Tail—Draw in feather outline. With Shader #10, shade from outer edge inward using Unbleached Titanium. Apply a wash of Raw Umber to soften.

Legs—Light orange. Mix Unbleached Titanium and Burnt Sienna.

Bill—Darker mix of leg color, black tip.

Spotted Sandpiper

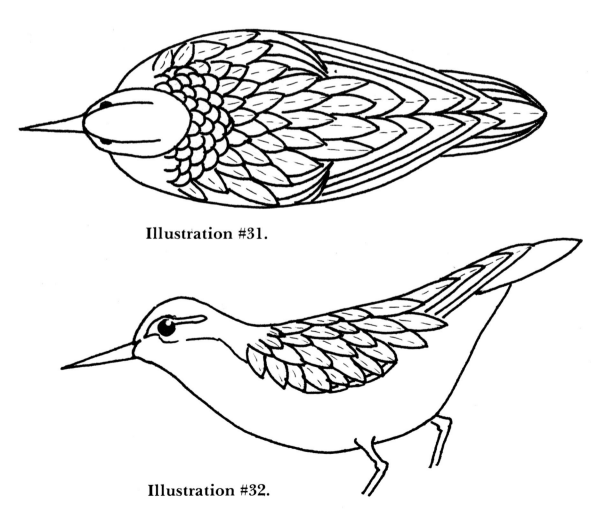

Illustration #31.

Illustration #32.

Dunlin

Illustration #33A.
Base Colors

Photo #36.

Photo #37.

Photo #38.

Photo #39.

Dunlin

Photo #40.

The Dunlin is a distinctive shorebird in breeding plumage and identification is easy by noting a bill slightly decurved toward the tip, a large black belly patch and black legs.

Large flocks may be seen flying in close formation and performing lightning quick directional changes of aerial aerobatics. They prefer the wet mud of estuaries for feeding; and the bill is used with a rapid "sewing machine" action to probe into the mud for the small creatures that make the mudflat their home.

Colors—Titanium White, Black, Unbleached Titanium, Raw Umber, Burnt Sienna, Yellow Ochre

Brushes—Liner #0, Shader #10, Kats Tongue #12, soft, round #10 Before beginning to paint, sand the carved blank to ensure that it is smooth. Apply a wood sealer to the entire blank and let dry. Apply a prime coat of paint, when dry lightly resand. See section on primers, page 16.

Draw in abstract areas and paint base colors as indicated. Refer to Illustration #33 and 33A.

Underbody—Refer to Illustrations #9 and 9A. Using a soft, round brush size 10, fan the brush until it has a "ragged" appearance. With Unbleached Titanium and beginning at the tail, make short sweeping feather-strokes (no more than 1/2" long) slightly angled inward at the center. Apply these strokes to the whole underside. Refer to Illustration #10. Apply a wash of Titanium White mixed with a very small amount of Unbleached Titanium. The Unbleached Titanium will prohibit a chalky look to the white. Refer to Illustration #11.

Repeat feather pattern and wash. Refer to Illustration #12.

Repeat feather pattern and wash. Refer to Illustration #13.

The whole underbody will be feathered white. This method of paint and wash application will achieve a soft, feathery appearance. Paint in black underbelly with Kats Tongue #12 using Dark Gray and the featherstroke technique. Refer to Illustrations #3 and 4 placing feathers close together.

Top and Head and Neck—Apply a base coat of thin Raw Umber. Draw in feather pattern on back using Liner #0. Refer to Illustration #34 and 35 as a guide. Highlight the feathers using Shader #10 with Unbleached Titanium. Stroke from outer edge inward on both the elongated and rounded feathers. Refer to Illustrations #14 thru 16. Apply a wash of thin Burnt Sienna. Repeat procedure until desired softness is

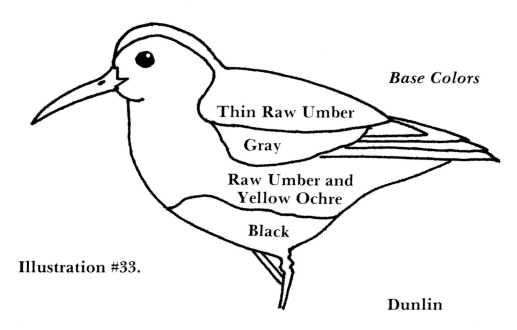

Illustration #33.

Base Colors

Thin Raw Umber

Gray

Raw Umber and Yellow Ochre

Black

Dunlin

achieved. Using Liner #0, stroke in airplane shaped areas with Black; paint from base of feather outward. Refer to Illustration #17 and Photo #40.

Side Pocket and Secondaries—Base coat area with medium gray mix of Black and Unbleached Titanium. Draw in feather pattern using Liner #0 with light gray paint. Highlight feathers using Shader #10 and light gray mix. To soften, apply a light gray wash. Refer to Photo #39.

Primaries—Base coat in Black. Highlight feathers with light gray mix. Stroke from outer edge inward. Apply a thin black wash to soften.

Tail—Base with a dark gray mix of Black with a touch of Unbleached Titanium. Draw in feather pattern with slightly lightened gray. Highlight the outer edge with Shader #10. Stroke from outside edge inward. Apply a thin black wash to soften.

Bill, Legs, Feet—Black

Illustration #34.
Dunlin

Illustration #35.

Golden Plover

Illustration #36A.
Base Colors

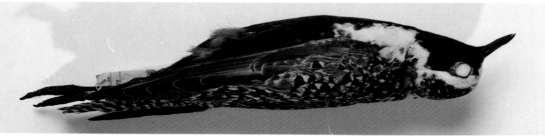

Photo #41.

Photo #42.

Photo #43.

Photo #44.

Golden Plover

Photo #45.

This beautiful shorebird nests in the high arctic tundra, so we seldom see it in its breeding plumage. With a striking black belly, it has a white head and side breast markings and a brownish back with golden highlights on the feathers. Habitat includes prairies, lake shores and mudflats. The diet mostly consists of insects, worms, berries, etc.

Colors—Titanium White, Black, Unbleached Titanium, Raw Umber, Yellow Ochre

Brushes—Liner #0, Shader #10, Kats Tongue #12, soft, round #10 Before beginning to paint, sand the carved blank to ensure that it is smooth. Apply a wood sealer to the entire blank and let dry. Apply a prime coat of paint, when dry lightly resand. See section on primers, page 16.

Draw in abstract areas and paint base colors as indicated. Refer to Illustration #36 and 36A. Paint white area around face and down to side breast.

Underbody and Face—Base color in black.

Using a soft, round brush size 10, fan the brush until it has a "ragged" appearance. With Dark Gray and beginning at the tail, make short sweeping featherstrokes (no more than 1/2" long) slightly angled inward at the center. Apply these strokes to the whole underside. Refer to Illustrations #9 thru 13 for technique. Apply a thin black wash. Repeat feather pattern and wash until desired softness is achieved.

Head and Back—Mix Black and Raw Umber for base color. Draw in feather pattern on back using Liner #0 with Dark Gray. Refer to Illustrations #37 and 38 as a guide. Highlight the outer edge of the rounded and elongated feathers with Dark Gray. Apply a thin coat of base color mix as a wash. Apply splotches of Yellow Ochre along edges of feathers. Apply splotches of white along outer edges of feathers. Refer to Photo #45.

Primaries—Base coat in Black. Highlight feathers with dark gray mix of Raw Umber and Unbleached Titanium, stroking from outer edge inward.

Tail—Barred black and white.

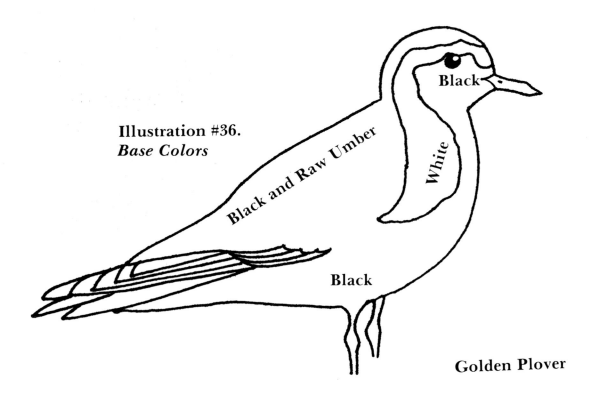

Illustration #36.
Base Colors

Black and Raw Umber

White

Black

Black

Golden Plover

Illustration #37.

Golden Plover

Illustration #38.

Avocet

Photo #46.

Photo #47.

Photo #48.

Photo #49.

Avocet
Illustration #39A.
Base Colors

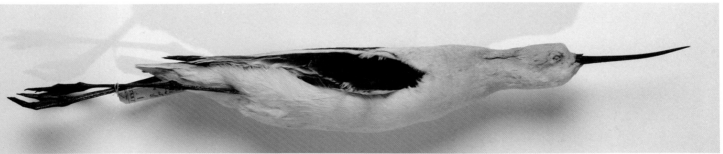

Photo #50.

Photo #51.

A very distinctive, stately and beautiful bird is the American Avocet. A thrilling sight to watch is an armada of these tall waders marching along in a shallow tidal estuary, swinging their heads from side to side in unison to catch the mud and water creatures in their path. The Avocet has very long blue-gray legs. In winter, the head is soft gray, turning to a beautiful salmon color in the spring as breeding season approaches. The other parts of the body have striking patterns of black and white. The bill of both male and female is recurved and the bill of the female is slightly more curved toward the tip. Jim, my husband, and I visited a nesting area for Avocets and Black Necked Stilts in the agricultural area of the Imperial Valley near El Centro, California. The bird population was so dense we had to be very careful to avoid stepping on the nests which were made of a few coarse sticks on the open ground. The birds are very protective of their nests and are quite fierce in defending their area.

Colors—Titanium white, Black, Unbleached Titanium, Raw Umber, Burnt Sienna, Ultramarine Blue, Yellow Ochre

Brushes—Liner #0, Shader #10, Kats Tongue #12, soft, round #10 Before beginning to paint, sand the carved blank to ensure that it is smooth. Apply a wood sealer to the entire blank and let dry. Apply a prime coat of paint, when dry lightly resand. See section on primers, page 16.

Draw in abstract areas and paint base colors as indicated, blending each color into the adjacent color. Refer to Illustration #39 and 39A.

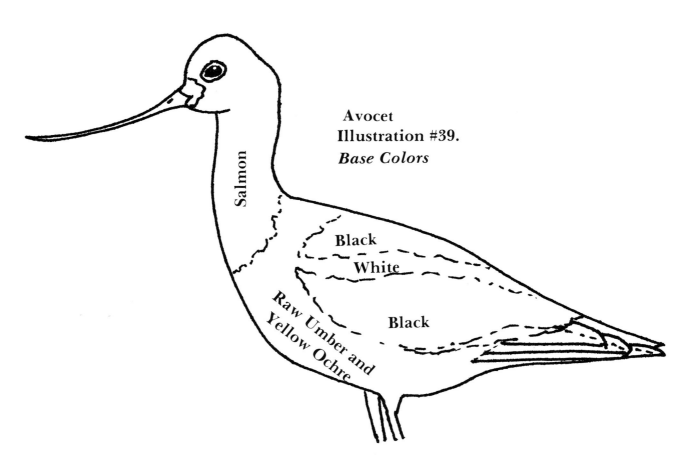

Avocet
Illustration #39.
Base Colors

Salmon

Black

White

Black

Raw Umber and Yellow Ochre

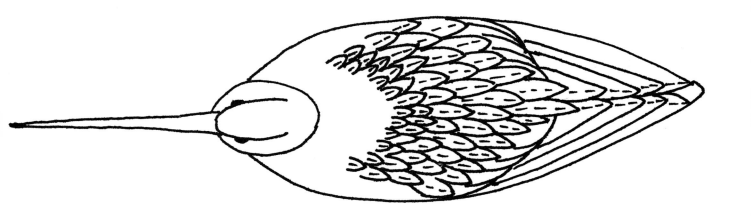

Illustration #40.

Avocet

Illustration #41.

Photo #52.

Avocet

Photo #53.

Avocet   Photo #54.

Underbody and White Feather Area of Back— Refer to Illustrations #9 and 9A. The base color is equal parts of Raw Umber and Yellow Ochre. Refer to Illustration #39A. Using a soft round brush, size 10, fan the brush until it has a "ragged" appearance. With Unbleached Titanium and beginning at the tail, make short sweeping feather-strokes (no more than 1/2" long) slightly angled inward at the center. Apply these strokes to the whole underside and white areas. Refer to Illustration #10. Apply a wash of Titanium White mixed with a very small amount of Unbleached Titanium. The Unbleached Titanium will prohibit a chalky look to the white. Refer to Illustration #11.

Repeat feather pattern and wash. Refer to Illustration #12.

Repeat feather pattern and wash. Refer to Illustration #13.

This method of paint and wash application will achieve a soft, feathery appearance.

Back—Draw in feather pattern using Liner #0 and gray paint. Refer to Illustrations #40 and 41 as a guide.

Black Feather Area of Back—Along front side pocket, shading would be a mix of Black and Raw Umber with a touch of Unbleached Titanium. Toward back of area, feathers are black at base and shaded from outside edge inward with a mix of Raw Umber and Unbleached Titanium. Use Shader #10. Refer to Photo #53.

Eye—White area around eye, also white area at back of bill shaded inward.

Bill—Black

Legs—Bluish gray; mix Black, Unbleached Titanium and a touch of Ultramarine Blue

Tail—Light gray with edges shaded in white.

Red Phalarope

A very small shorebird that generally inhabits the open ocean when not nesting is the Red Phalarope. However, during migration, I have seen flocks of several hundred in a brine shrimp pond near my home. They are also found on inland waters and tidal marshes. Frequently, they swim in tight circles, spinning repeatedly.

The female is a truly liberated bird. She is the aggressor in courting, defends the homestead and has a more brilliant coat than the male. When she lays her eggs, her job is over. The male incubates the eggs and raises the young.

Colors—Titanium White, Black, Unbleached Titanium, Raw Umber, Yellow Ochre, Burnt Sienna, Cadmium Yellow Medium, Cadmium Red Medium.

Brushes—Liner #0, Shader #10, Kats Tongue #12, soft, round #10 Before beginning to paint, sand the carved blank to ensure that it is smooth. Apply a wood sealer to the entire blank and let dry. Apply a prime coat of paint, when dry lightly resand. See section on primers, page 16.

Draw in abstract areas and paint base colors as indicated, blending each color into the adjacent color. Refer to Illustration #42 and 42A.

Underbody, Breast and Neck—Base color in light Burnt Sienna. Stroke on feather pattern with thin Unbleached Titanium. Apply a Burnt Sienna wash. Refer to

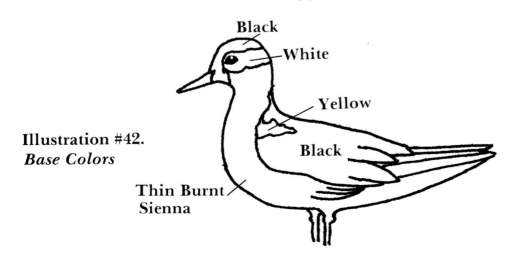

Illustration #42.
Base Colors

Black

White

Yellow

Black

Thin Burnt Sienna

Illustration #42A.
Base Colors

Red Phalarope

Photo #55.

Photo #56.

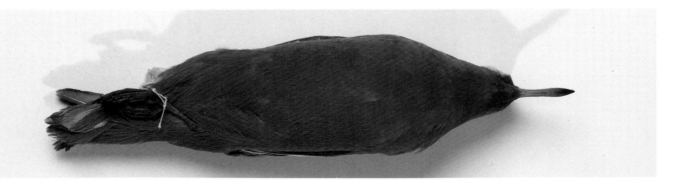

Photo #57.

Photo #58.

Red Phalarope

Photo #59.

Illustrations #10 thru 13 for technique. Repeat procedure until desired softness is achieved.

Back—Draw in feather pattern using Liner #0 and gray. Refer to Illustrations #43 and 44 as a guide. Shade in from base of feather toward tip with mixture of Yellow Ochre and a touch of Cadmium Yellow Medium. Refer to Photos #58 and 59.

Primaries—Black. Outer edge shaded with Yellow Ochre and a touch of Unbleached Titanium.

Tail—Black, shaded with gray

Top of Head and Face—Black

Side Face—White

Bill—Cadmium Yellow Medium with a touch of Unbleached Titanium

Illustration #43.

Red Phalarope   **Illustration #44.**

Woodcock

Many people think that the Woodcock is a gamebird; but in truth, it is classified as a shorebird. This bird is a master of camouflage and until disturbed, is rarely seen. They inhabit the eastern part of North America and the feather markings are not similar to other species. Earthworms are the main diet food, so the habitat in which they thrive must be rich, moist soil in order to probe for their favorite food.

The feather pattern of a Woodcock is intricate and difficult. This is a simplified version.

Colors—Titanium White, Black, Unbleached Titanium, Raw Umber, Burnt Sienna, Paynes Gray

Brushes—Liner #0, Shader #10, Kats Tongue #12, soft, round #10 Before beginning to paint, sand the carved blank to ensure that it is smooth. Apply a wood sealer to the entire blank and let dry. Apply aprime coat of paint, when dry lightly resand. See section on primers, page 16.

Draw in abstract areas and paint base colors as indicated, blending each color into

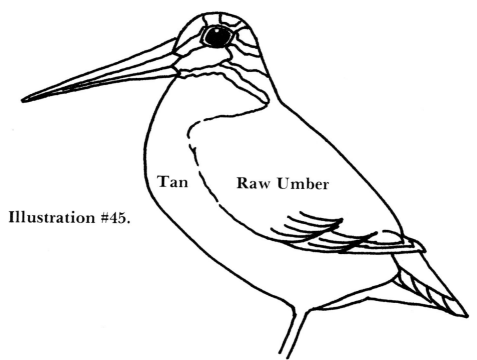

Illustration #45.

Tan   Raw Umber

Raw Umber

Woodcock
Illustration #45A.
Base Colors

Tan Base Coat

Illustration #46.

Yellow Ochre + Burnt Sienna   **+ Unbleached Titanium = Base Coat**

Photo #60.

Photo #61.

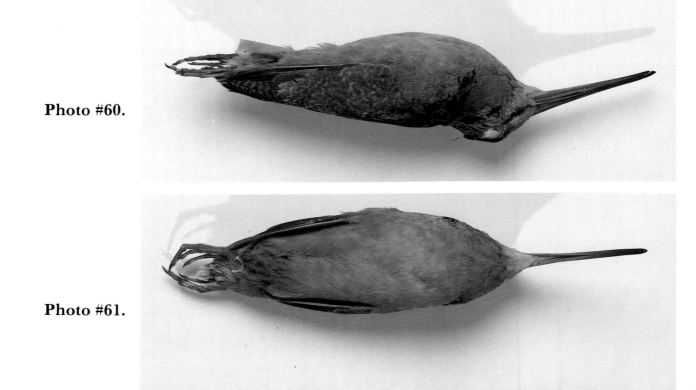

Photo #62.

Photo #63.

Woodcock

Photo #64.

the adjacent color. Refer to Illustration #45 and 45A.

Underbody—Mix Unbleached Titanium, Yellow Ochre and a touch of Burnt Sienna for base coat. Refer to Illustration #46. Apply feather pattern using a soft, round #10 and thin Raw Umber. Refer to Illustrations #10 thru 13 for technique. Apply a thin wash of basemix. Repeat procedure until desired softness is achieved. Refer to Illustrations #10 thru 13 for technique.

Back, Wings and Tail—Draw in feather pattern using Liner #0 and black paint. Refer to Illustrations #47 and 48 as a guide. For the rounded head and shoulder feathers, use Kats Tongue #12 with Unbleached Titanium. Stroke from outer edge inward on both the rounded and elongated feathers.

Apply a wash of Raw Umber to soften. Repeat procedure until desired softness is achieved. Paint in blue-gray feathers with a mixture of Paynes Gray and Unbleached Titanium. Refer to Photo #64.

Top of Head—Paint Unbleached Titanium, Black and Raw Umber bars across crown blending each color into the next.

Cheek Detail—Using Liner #0, stroke Unbleached Titanium and Raw Umber detail lines, blending the strokes.

Eye—Brown with White ring

Bill—Unbleached Titanium and touch of Burnt Sienna. Black tip.

Feet—Grayish tan. Mix Unbleached Titanium with a touch of Raw Umber.

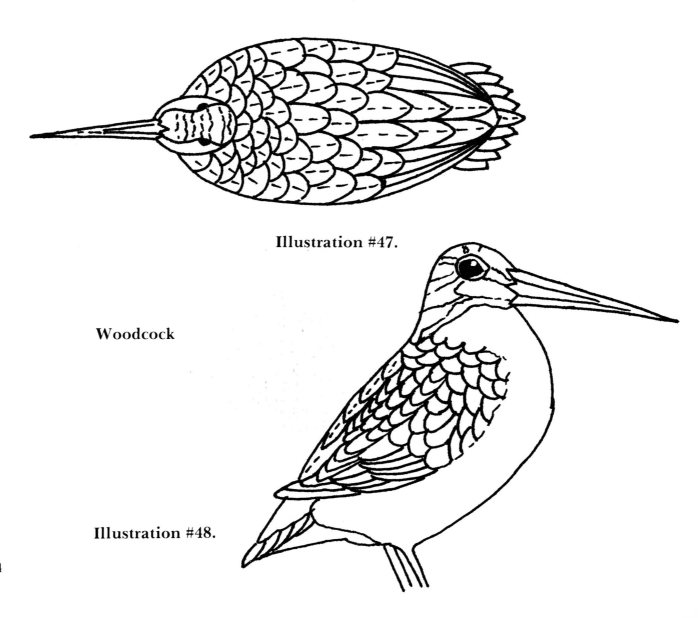

Illustration #47.

Woodcock

Illustration #48.

History of Decoy Carving

Of the many types of American folk art—weathervanes, cigar store Indians, barbershop poles—perhaps the most original is the decoy. Defined by the World Book Dictionary as "an artificial bird used to lure birds into a trap or within gunshot," the decoy has maintained its allure for sportsmen, collectors and artisans for centuries.

In 1924, an archeological discovery in Lovelock Cave, Nevada revealed a beautifully preserved group of decoys dating back more than a thousand years. Several of them, cleverly depicting the canvasback duck, were made of woven tule grass colored with the dyes that the American Indians made from natural substances. Indians used white feathers along the sides of the decoy to provide a realistic look to the form. The whole body was then bound with a fine cord or line. These ancient decoys are on display at the North American Indian Museum in New York City and were the beginning of the art form as we know it today.

Early settlers in America depended upon wild game for food and found many uses for the feathers of wildfowl. They took their cue from the Indians and fashioned decoys to draw waterfowl into close range of both gun and arrow.

The growing population in America led to the inception of market hunting. This new breed of hunter killed and sold wild game birds to the general population. They utilized large numbers of decoys in their "rigs," enabling them to mass kill anything on the wing to fill orders for the growing market. No bird was exempt; songbirds, waterfowl and shorebirds were all included. Because of the increasing number of decoys demanded for the market hunter's rigs, and the amount of time required to carve a decoy, the hand carvers were no longer able to keep up with production. American ingenuity soon produced the first factory-made decoys and a new business was born. Decoys were manufactured by the thousands to provide for the "market hunters" as well as for the sportsman. Today, these machine-made birds are highly valued as collector's items. Decoys manufactured by Mason, Evans, Pratt, Stevens, and others bring tremendous prices at decoy auctions.

In 1918, the Congress of the United States passed the Migratory Bird Treaty Act, which outlawed the killing of migratory birds. With the passage of the act, the demand for factory-made decoys declined rapidly. In recent years, however, the machine-made birds have made a comeback and the business of manufacturing decoys is thriving again. In addition to birds used by sportsmen for their shooting rigs, there is a new market for artists, craftsmen, and tole and decorative painters. Carvers and artists enhance the basic decoy by painting, woodburning feather patterns and inserting feathers to make the wooden blanks look more realistic.

During both the rise and the fall in popularity of the machine-made bird, hand-made decoys continued to be crafted for carvers' own collections and small commercial demand. Many of these old time carvers are now considered to be the "Old Masters" of American folk art and their works are prized and sought after by collectors. Elmer Crowell, Nathan Cobb, Joe Lincoln, Charles Wheeler, Charles Perdew, Bill Bowman, Harry Shourds, and Steve and Lem Ward are a few of the most notable carvers from this era.

The Chesapeake Bay and surrounding areas were and still are considered one of the prime waterfowl areas for hunters and bird watchers alike. In the early 1900s in the eastern shore town of Crisfield, Maryland, Steve and Lem Ward were barbers who spent their off-time carving decoys. Generally, Steve did the carving and Lem did the painting. Through the years, they pioneered the evolution from functional decoys to the more current decorative poses. They inserted feathers and gave their birds legs to better express and add realism to their craft. The Ward brothers carved for over fifty years and produced approximately 25,000 decoys. After the death of Steve in 1976, Lem continued painting, drawing and writing poetry until his death in 1984. The collection of a serious decoy enthusiast would not be complete without a Ward Brothers decoy.

The Ward Foundation

The Ward Foundation, named for Steve and Lem Ward, was established in 1958 to promote and perpetuate interest in wildlife art and carving and the conservation of both wildlife and natural resources. As an outgrowth of the Ward Foundation, the North American Wildlife Art Museum was established at Salisbury State College in Salisbury, Maryland in 1975. Over 3000 carvings and artifacts are on display at the museum, which follow the progress of decoy carving from the beginning of the art form to the present.

The Ward Foundation began the World Championship Carving Competition in 1971. The competition moved from Salisbury, Maryland in 1979 and is now held on the last weekend in April each year at Convention Hall in Ocean City, Maryland. Approximately 2500 different carvings are entered in competition each year, representing the work of about 800 to 900 carvers from across the United States and Canada. The World Championship Carving Competition is considered to be one of the most prestigious shows for carvers and the competition is intense.

The Waterfowl Festival

Easton, Maryland, home of the Waterfowl Festival, is a charming town of only 8000 residents with quaint shops, colonial architecture and the warmth common to the people of the eastern shore. In 1971, through the efforts of two Easton residents, Dr. Harry M. Walsh and Bill Perry, the Waterfowl Festival was born. Through the foresight and determination of these two men, the Waterfowl Festival has developed into the largest and most prestigious show of its kind in the nation.

Today more than 700 dedicated volunteers share in the preparation and staging of this tribute to wildfowl. Profits from this enormous effort are contributed to various wildlife organizations for the conservation and preservation of our natural resources and wildlife habitat. Held on the second weekend of November each year, the very top names in waterfowl art—carvers, painters, sculptors, photographers, and collectors—are invited to participate in this show.

During the event, Easton hosts more than 20,000 visitors, who tour the different exhibit areas via free shuttle buses or on foot, directed by flying geese graphics that volunteers have painted on the sidewalks.

The Tidewater Inn serves as headquarters for the Waterfowl Festival and houses the Gold Room, where the finest waterfowl art is displayed. The carvings displayed in the Armory are so lifelike, they seem as if they may take flight at any moment. Wildfowl photography is exhibited at the Academy of Arts and the firehouse is home for the workshop, where carvers and artists demonstrate their crafts. Other attractions include gift shops, book corners, artifact exhibits, buy, sell and swap areas, a duck and goose calling contest and an auction of antique decoys. The collector, artist, nature enthusiast or home shopper is sure to find excitement and perhaps a few treasures at the Waterfowl Festival.

Glossary of Bird Definitions

Barbs—the part of the feather attached to the quill

Breast—front chest of bird

Coverts—feathers at the base of the upper tail, also at the base of underneath tail area

Crest—long feathers at the base of the head and neck

Crown—forehead and top of bird's head

Eye Trough—a recessed area in the front and back of the eye

Iridescence—shimmering metallic colors on feathers

Jowl—jutting part of the jaw

Primaries—the ten largest flight feathers of the wing

Secondaries—the ten small feathers of the inner wing

Side Pocket—Recessed area between side and back of bird

Tertials—larger feathers of the inner wing

Vermiculation—winding and wavy lines like the tracks of worms (Webster) that appear on the feathers of many species of wildfowl

Bibliography

Audubon Society Book of Waterbirds

Audubon Society Waterbird Guide

Carlson & Binford—*Birds of Western North America*

Hayman, Marchant, Prater—*Shorebirds, An Identification Guide*

Johnsgard—*The Plovers, Sandpipers and Snipes of the World*

Landsdowne—*Birds of the Northern Forest*

Landsdowne—*Birds of the Eastern Forest, Volume 1*

Landsdowne—*Birds of the West Coast, Vols. 1 & 2*

Matthiessen & Clem—*Shorebirds of North America*

Peterson—*A Field Guide to Birds*

Reference Books

ALLEN, BONNIE—*Songbird Patterns*
ALLEN, BONNIE—*Songbird Patters Book #2*
BARBER, GEO. & READER, LARRY—*Decoy Carving Techniques for the Intermediate Carver*
BASILE, KENNETH & DOERZBACH, CYNTHIA—*American Decorative Bird Carving*
BERRY, BOB—*Decoy Patterns by Bob Berry*
BERRY, BOB—*How To Carve Fish*
BOWEN, FREDDIE—*Decorative Duck Painting (color charts)*
BRIDENHAGEN, KEITH & SPEILMAN, PATRICK—*Realistic Decoys, Carving, Texturing, Painting and Finishing*
BRIDENHAGEN, KEITH—*Decoy Pattern Book*
BURK, BRUCE—*Complete Waterfowl Studies, 3 Volumes*   Volume 1—Dabbling Ducks and Whistling Ducks   Volume 2—Diving Ducks   Volume 3—Geese and Swans
BURK, BRUCE—*Game Bird Carving, New Revised Edition*
BURK, BRUCE—*Waterfowl Studies*
BURK, BRUCE—*Decorative Decoy Designs*
CASSEDY, ED & CLODFELTER, KEN—*Carve-It, How to carve a Green Winged Teal*
CASSON, PAUL W.—*Decoys Simplified*
CHAPEL & SULLIVAN—*Wildlife Woodcarvers*
CONNETT, EUGENE—*Duck Decoys, How to Make Them, How to Paint Them, How To Rig Them*
DAISEY & KURMAN—*Songbird Carving #1*
DAISEY & KURMAN—*Songbird Carving #2*
FRANK, CHARLES W. JR.—*Anatomy of a Waterfowl for Carvers and Painters*
GILLEY, WENDELL—*Art of Bird Carving*
GODIN, PAT—*Championship Waterfowl Patterns, Vol. 1*

GODIN, PAT—*Championship Waterfowl Patterns, Vol. 2*
GREEN, H.D.—*Carving Realistic Birds*
GREEN, H.D.—*Patterns and Instructions for Carving Authentic Birds*
GUGE, BOB—*Carving Miniature Wildfowl with Bob Guge*
GUGE, BOB—*Carving Miniature Wildfowl*
HILLMAN, ANTHONY—*Painting Duck Decoys*
HILLMAN, ANTHONY—*Carving Classic Regional Shorebirds*
HILLMAN, ANTHONY—*Carving Classic Swan and Goose Decoys*
HOLLATZ, TOM & DWYER, CORINE—*The Loon Book*
HOPPER, BEEBE—*Featherstrokes, The Basic of Feather Painting*
HOPPER, BEEBE—*Featherstrokes for Canvasbacks*
HOPPER, BEEBE—*Featherstrokes for Mallards*
HOPPER, BEEBE—*Wildfowl Painting*
HOPPER, BEEBE—*Painting Wild Geese*
HAUSER, PRISCILLA—*Decorative Ducks*
HAUSER, PRISCILLA—*Decorative Ducks Volume #2*
KLEIN, TOM—*Loon Magic*
LADD, DAVE—*Creative Woodburning #11*
LADD, DAVE—*Wooden Ducks, An Artist's Portfolio*
LEHMAN, GEORGE—*20 Realistic Game & Songbird Wood Carving Patterns*
LEHMAN, GEORGE—*Realism In Wood*
LEHMAN, GEORGE—*Nature In Wood*
LEMASTER, RICHARD—*Decoys: The Art of the Wooden Bird*
LEMASTER, RICHARD—*Waterfowl—The Artists' Guide to Anatomy, Attitude and Color*
LEMASTER, RICHARD—*Wildlife In Wood*
LEMASTER, RICHARD—*Great Gallery of Ducks*
MOHRDART, DAVID—*Bird Reference Drawings*
MOHRDART, DAVID—*Selected Bird Drawings*
MOHRDART, DAVID—*Bird Studies*
MUEHLMATT, ERNIE—*Songbird Carving with Ernest Muehlmatt*
MUEHLMATT, ERNIE—*Songbird Carving*
MURPHY, CHARLES F.—*Working Plans: Kit #1*
MURPHY, CHARLES F.—*Working Plans: Kit #2*
PHILLIPS, JOHN CHARLES—*A Natural History of the Ducks*
PLAUMANN, FRED—*Selected Bird Patterns for Carvers, Vols. 1 & 2*
PONTE, ALFRED M.—*Decoy Sculptures In Wood*
PONTE, ALFRED M.—*26 Realistic Duck Patterns*
SMALL, ANNE—*Masters of Bird Carving*
SCHROEDER, ROGER—*How To Carve Wildfowl #1*
SCHROEDER, ROGER—*How To Carve Wildfowl #2*
SCHROEDER, ROGER—*Waterfowl Carving with J.D. Sprankle*
SHEELER, JOHN—*Bird Carver*
SHOURDS, HARRY V. & HILLMAN, ANTHONY—*Carving Duck*

Decoys, with full size patterns for hollow construction

SHOURDS, HARRY V. & HILLMAN, ANTHONY—*Carving Shorebirds*

SHOURDS, HARRY V. & HILLMAN, ANTHONY—*Exotic Decoys for the Woodcarver*

SPIELMAN, PATRICK—*Making Wood Decoys*

STARR, DR. GEORGE R.—*How To Make Working Decoys*

SULLIVAN, CLARK & CHAPPEL—*Wildlife Wood Carvers Pattern Book, Drake Puddle Ducks*

TODD, FRANK S.—*Waterfowl, Ducks, Geese and Swans of the World*

VEASEY, WILLIAM—*Waterfowl Carving, Blue Ribbon Techniques*

VEASEY, WILLIAM—*Waterfowl Painting, Blue Ribbon Techniques*

VEASEY, WILLIAM—*Blue Ribbon Burning Techniques*

VEASEY, WILLIAM & SINA, KURMAN—*Bills and Feet, An Artisan's Handbook*

VEASEY, TRICIA—*Waterfowl Illustrated*

VEASEY, TRICIA & JOHNSON, TOM—*Championship Carving*

WYLIE, STEPHEN & FURLONG, STEWARD—*Key to North American Waterfowl*

Reference Journals

Wildfowl Art, Journal of the Ward Foundation
655 S. Salisbury Blvd.
Salisbury, MD 21801

Decoy Magazine
P.O. Box 1900
Montego Bay Station
Ocean City, MD 21842

Wildlife Art News
P.O. Box 237
Elk River, MN 55330

Wildfowl Carving and Collecting
P.O. Box 1831
Cameron and Kelker Sts.
Harrisburg, PA 17105

Breakthrough
P.O. Box 1320
Loganville, GA 30249

Decoy Hunter
901 North 9th
Clinton, IN 47842

Birder's World
720 E. 8th Street
Holland, MI 49423

WildBird
P.O. Box 483
Mt. Morris, IL 61054-0483

Exhibits, Shows and Competitions

There are many bird carving and art shows, both exhibition and competition, all across the nation. Today, one remark that is heard at many competitive shows is, "Don't put a live bird in the tank, he might come in second place!"

The first shows began about thirty-five years ago in the east. Today, many municipalities and organizations promote a bird carving and art show. Most of them are still concentrated in the eastern region of the country, but other areas are now privileged to host these events.

Canada produces many top award winning and enthusiastic carvers. This international participation is enjoyed by most of the larger shows. Canada stages several very fine waterfowl shows each year. Word from England is that bird carving is slowly progressing there.

Some of the finest bird carvers in the nation are from Michigan, which hosts some top shows. Louisiana has fine shows. California has two shows each year; mid-February the Pacific Southwest Wildfowl Arts promotes a major show in San Diego; Sacramento has the Pacific Flyway Decoy Show in late June. New York, Alabama, Ohio, New Jersey, North Carolina, South Carolina, Maryland and Virginia are just a few of the states where major shows are held.

Following is a partial listing of shows and cities in which they are held.

JANUARY

FEBRUARY

Minnesota Decoy Collectors Show
St. Paul, Minnesota

California Open Wildfowl Arts Festival
San Diego, California

Long Island Decoy Collectors
East Setauket, New York

Wildfowl Carving and Art Exhibition
Richmond, Virginia

Southeastern Wildlife Exposition
Charleston, South Carolina

Manasquan River Decoy Show
Wall Township, New Jersey

MARCH

Canadian National Decoy Carvers
   Competition
Toronto, Ontario, Canada

Quebec Waterfowl Carving Contest
Montreal, Quebec, Canada

Woodcarving and Wildlife Art Festival
Lancaster, Pennsylvania

Mid Atlantic Wildfowl Festival
Virginia Beach, Virginia

Delaware Wildlife Art Show
Newark, Delaware

Northeastern Wildlife Exhibition
Albany, New York

U. S. National Decoy Show
Melville, New York

Chincoteague Island Easter Decoy Festival
Chincoteague, Virginia

Wisconsin Decoy Collectors Show
Oshkosh, Wisconsin

Ohio Decoy Collectors and Carvers Show
Westlake, Ohio

National Wildlife Art Show
Overland Park, Kansas

Annapolis Wildfowl Carving and Art
   Exhibition
Annapolis, Maryland

Mid-Atlantic Wildfowl Festival
Virginia Beach, Virginia

Michigan Wildlife Art Festival
Southfield, Michigan

APRIL

Ward Foundation World's Championship
Wildfowl Carving Competition
Ocean City, Maryland

Mid-Atlantic Woodcarving Show and
   Competition
Abington, Pennsylvania

Waterfowl and Wildlife Decoy Show and
   Competition
Toms River, New Jersey

Michigan Wildlife Art Festival
Southfield, Michigan

National Antique Decoy Collectors Show
St. Charles, Illinois

Wild Birds in Wood
Portland, Oregon

Texas Wildfowl Art and Antique Festival
Dallas, Texas

Midwest Decoy Collectors Association
Chicago, Illinois

MAY

South Jersey Woodcarving Show
Millville, New Jersey

Muleskinner Decoy Show
Clarence, New York

Havre de Grace Decoy Festival
Havre de Grace, Maryland

JUNE

Pacific Flyway Decoy Association Wildfowl
  Festival
Sacramento, California

Susquehanna Decoy Shop Outdoor
  Woodcarving Show
Intercourse, Pennsylvania

Toronto Decoy Show
Toronto, Ontario, Canada

Ontario Decoy Show
Oshawa, Ontario

JULY

New England Decoy Association
Hyannis, Massachusetts

Cape May Waterfowl and Woodcarving
  Show
Cape May, New Jersey

Clayton Duck Decoy and Wildlife Art Show
Clayton, New York

AUGUST

Canadian Agricultural International
  Woodcarving Exhibition
Toronto, Ontario, Canada

Cajun Hunters Festival and Waterfowl
  Carving Competition
Galliano, Louisiana

Buckhorn Wildlife Art Festival
Buckhorn, Ontario, Canada

International Decoy Contest
Davenport, Iowa

Northwoods Decoy Collectors Show
Minocqua, Wisconsin

West Coast Antique Decoy Collectors
  Show and Sale
Monterey, California

SEPTEMBER

Cape Cod Annual Carvers Exhibit
Brewster, Massachusetts

Old Time Barnegat Bay Decoy and
   Gunning Show
Tuckerton, New Jersey

Yorkarvers Woodcarving and Decoy Show
York, Pennsylvania

Louisiana Wildfowl Festival
New Orleans, Louisiana

North American Wildfowl Carving
   Championships
Livonia, Michigan

Michigan Duck Hunters Tournament
   and Decoy Contest
Pointe Mouille, Michigan

Eddie Bauer Wildlife Art and Carvers Show
Seattle, Washington

Leigh Yawkey Woodson Art Museum
Wausau, Wisconsin

OCTOBER

Ward Foundation Wildfowl Carving
   and Art Exhibition
Salisbury, Maryland

Kingsfield-Gosfield South Migratory
   Festival
Kingsville, Ontario, Canada

Chestertown Wildlife Show
Chestertown, Maryland

Currituck Wildlife Festival
Barco, North Carolina

Catahoula Lake Festival
Pineville, Louisiana

North Carolina Waterfowl Weekend
Nags Head, North Carolina

NOVEMBER

Easton Waterfowl Festival
Easton, Maryland

Bird Carvers Exhibition and Sale
Worchester, Massachusetts

Pennsylvania Wildlife Art Festival
York, Pennsylvania

Southern Wildfowl Festival
Decatur, Alabama

Wildfowl West Festival
San Bernardino, California

DECEMBER

Pennsylvania Wildlife Arts Festival
York, Pennsylvania

Sources for Materials

A Change of Scene
John and Orchid Davis
P.O. Box 381
Westminster, SC 29693
(manzanita bases)

Al's Decoy Supplies
27 Connaught Ave.
London, Ont., Canada
N5Y 3A4
(misc. supplies)

American Sales Company
Box 741
Reseda, CA 91335
(misc. supplies)

Annex Manufacturing
955 Blue Ball Rd.
Elkton, MD 21921
(Wood burners)

Atlantic Flyway Decoy Co.
2248 Seashore Shoppes
Great Neck and Shore Dr.
Virginia Beach, VA 23451
(misc. supplies)

Avian Art, Inc.
4288 Staunton Dr.
Swartz Creek, MI 48473
(books, videos)

Birds of A Feather
Box 756
New Britain, CT 06050
(wooden bases)

Big Sky Carvers
8256 Huffine Lane
Bozeman, MT 59715
(machine blanks)

Bob Bolle
26421 Compson
Roseville, MI 48066
(Cast Study bills)

Books Plus
42 Charles St.
Lodi, NJ 07644
(books)

Buck Run Carving Supply
151 Gully Road
Aurora, NY 13026
(misc. supplies)

Canadian Woodworker, Ltd.
1391 St. James St.
Winnepeg, Manitoba, Canada
R3H 0Z1
(misc. supplies)

Carvers Corner
153 Passaic St.
Garfield, NJ 07026
(misc. supplies)

Carvers' Eye
P.O. Box 16692
Portland, OR 97216
(glass eyes)

Chesterfield Craft Shop
P.O. Box 208
Chesterfield, NJ 08620
(misc supplies, burners, feet)

Chez La Rogue
Rt. 3, Box 148
Foley, AL 36535
(misc. supplies)

Colwood Electronics
1 Meridian Rd.
Eatontown, NJ 07724
(wood burners)

Albert Constantine & Sons
2050 Eastchester Rd.
Bronx, NY 10461
(misc. supplies)

Craft Cove, Inc.
2315 West Glen Ave.
Peoria, IL 61614
(misc. supplies)

Craftwoods
10921 York Rd.
Hunt Valley, MD 21030
(misc. supplies)

Curt's Waterfowl Corner
123 Le Boeuf St.
Montegut, LA 70377
(misc. supplies)

Decoy Carving Supplies
59 Woodcrest Ave.
St. Albert, Alb. Canada
T8N 3H8
(Misc. supplies)

Richard Delise
920 Springwood Dr.
West Chester, PA 19380
(cast feet)

Dolington Woodcrafts
Washington Crsg & Newtown
Rd.
Newtown, PA 18940
(machine blanks)

The Duck Blind
8721-B Gull Rd.
Richland, MI 49083
(videos, misc. supplies)

The Duck Butt Boys
P.O. Box 2051
Metairie, LA 70004
(wood)

Electric Tool Service Co.
19442 Conant Ave.
Detroit, MI 48234
(misc. supplies)

P.C. English Enterprises
P.O. Box 380, 6201 Mallard Rd.
Thornburg, VA 22401
(supermarket for wood carvers)

Exotic Woods, Inc.
2483 Industrial St.
Burlington, Ont, Canada
L7P 1A6
(misc. supplies)

The Eyes
9630 Dundalk
Spring, TX 77379
(glass eyes)

Feather Merchants
279 Boston Post Rd.
Madison, CT 06443
(misc. supplies)

The Fine Tool Shops, Inc.
P.O. Box 1262
Danbury, CT 06810
(misc. supplies)

Elkay Products Co.
1506 Sylvan Glade
Austin, TX 78745
(ruby cutters)

Foredom Electric Co.
Rt. 6
Bethel, CT 05801
(Foredom tool)

Forest Products
P.O. Box 12
Avon, OH 44011
(machine blanks)

Georgetown, Inc.
P.O. Box 625
Bethel Park, PA 15012
(video tapes)

Gerry's Tool Shed
1111 Flint Rd., Unit 6
Downsview, Ont., Canada
M3J 3C7
(misc. supplies)

Gesswein
255 Hancock Ave.
Bridgeport, CT 06605
(Power Carver)

Godin Art., Inc.
P.O. Box 62
Brantford, Ont., Can.
N3T 5N3
(books, videos, Study Kast)

Greenwing Enterprises
Rt. 2, Box 731-B
Chester, MD 21619
(molded birds, books videos)

John E. Heintz
6609 S. River Rd.
Marine City, MI 48039
(wildfowl photos)

Highwood Farms Book Shop
P.O. Box 1246
Traverse City, MI 49648
(books)

Beebe and Jim Hopper
731 Beech Avenue
Chula Vista, CA 92010
(Permalba paints, Langnickel
brushes, videos, books)

Christian J. Hummel Co.
404 Brooklets Ave.
Easton, MD 21601
(art supplies)

Jennings Decoy Co.
Dept. WF, 30 Lincoln Ave. NE
St. Cloud, MN 56301
(decoys)

Oscar Johnson
Rt. 2, Box 1224
Smith River, CA 95567
(reference posters, study bills)

Kulis Karvit
725 Broadway Ave.
Bedford, OH 44146
(epoxy putty)

J.H. Kline Carving Shop
Rt.2, Forge Hill Rd.
Manchester, PA 17345
(misc. supplies)

Knotts Knives
7 Blue Acres Rd.
Middletown, CT 06457
(knives)

Lee Valley Tools, Ltd.
2680 Queensview Dr.
Ottawa, Ont., Canada
K2B 8J9
(misc. tools)

Leisure Time Products, Inc.
2650 Davisson St., WF-1
River Grove, IL 60171
(wood burner)

Lewis Tools & Supply Co.
912 West 8th St.
Loveland, CO 80537
(misc. supplies)

Little Mountain Carving
Rt. 5, Box 563
Winchester, VA 22601
(misc. supplies)

Lominak Knives
P.O. Box 1189
Abingdon, VA 24210
(Knives)

Louisiana Swamp Wood
Rt. 5 W, Box 1577-A
St. Francisville, LA 70775
(wood)

Makepeace
1482 Maple Ave.
Paoli, PA 19301
(knives)

Master Paint Systems
P.O. Box 1320
Loganville, GA 30249
(misc. supplies)

Bob Miller
General Delivery
Evergreen, LA 71333
(Cast study bills)

Montana Decoy Co.
Rt. 1, Box 251
Wilsall, MT 59086
(misc. supplies)

Ernie Muehlmatt
700 Old Marple Rd.
Springfield, PA 19064
(cast study birds)

Northwest Carving Supplies
P.O. Box 407, Dept. WFF
Manhattan, MT 59741
(misc. supplies)

Ole Tollers
P.O. Box 761
La Jolla, CA 92038
(antique decoys)

Rioux's
P.O. Box 3008WF
Syracuse, NY 13220-3008
(display cases)

Ritter Carvers, Inc.
1559 Dillon Rd.
Maple Glen, PA 19002
(misc. supplies)

Ross Tool Co.
257 Queen St., West
Toronto, Ont., Canada
M5V 1Z4
(misc. supplies)

SMC Enterprises
RR #3, Box 72B
Browerville, MN 56438
(dustsucker)

Sand-Rite Manufacturing Co.
1611 N. Sheffield Ave.
Chicago, IL 60614
(sanders)

Schoepfer Eyes
W. 31st St.
New York, NY 10001
(glass eyes)

Seto Co., Inc.
P.O. Box 148, 195 Hwy. 36
West Keansbury, NJ 07734
(misc. supplies)

Robert J. Smith
14900 W. 31st Ave.
Golden, CO 80401
(glass eyes)

Larry Stevens
3005 Pine Spring Rd.
Falls Church, VA 22042
(wildfowl photos)

Gordon Stiller
155 Superior St.
Omro, WI 54963
(patterns)

Susquehanna Decoy Shop
Kitchen Kettle Village
Intercourse, PA 17354
(misc. supplies)

David Taylor
78 Grove St.
So. Braintree, MA 02184
(cast feet)

Taylormade Bird Feet
78 Grove Street
Braintree, MA 02184
(cast feet)

Tohickson Glass Eyes
P.O. Box 15
Erwinna, PA 021284
(glass eyes)

Tool Bin
10575 Clark Rd.
Browerville, MN 56438
(misc. tools)

Veasey Studios
955 Blue Ball Rd.
Elkton, MD 21921
(misc. supplies, books)

Joe Veracke and Associates
P.O. Box 48962
Chicago, IL 60648
(misc. tools)

Video Communications
318 Wellington
Traverse City, MI 49684
(videos)

Garret Wade
161 Avenue of the Americas
New York, NY 10013
(misc. tools)

Warren Tool Co.
Rt. 1, 14AS
Rhinebeck, NY 12572
(misc. tools)

Richard Watson
8800 Anchor Bay
Fair Haven, MI 48023
(Misc. Supplies)

Welbeck Sawmill Ltd.
RR 2
Durham, Ont. Canada
N0G 1R0
(woods)

Wil-Cut Company
7113 Spicer Drive
Citrus Heights, CA 95621
(misc. supplies)

Wildlife Artists Supply Co.
360 Hwy. 78, P.O. Box 1330WC
Loganville, GA 30249
(misc. supplies)

Wildlife Arts and Crafts
102 Wildlife Lane
Salisbury, MD 21801
(bases)

Wildlife Carving Supply
317 Holyoke Ave.
Beach Haven, NJ 08008
(misc. supplies)

Wildlife Woodcarvers
4288 Staunton Dr.
Swartz Creek, MI 48473
(misc. supplies)

Woodcraft Shop
2724 State St.
Bettendorf, IA 52722
(misc. supplies)

Woodcarvers Supply, Inc.
926-D W. Oceanview Ave.
Norfolk, VA 23503
(misc. supplies)

Woodcarvers Supply Co.
41 Atlantic Ave.
Woburn, MA 01888
(misc. supplies)

Wood Carvers Supply Co.
3056 Excelsior Blvd.
Minneapolis, MN 55416
(misc. supplies)

Wood N' Things, Inc.
601 E 44th St., #3
Boise, ID 83714
(misc. supplies)

Woodworkers Choice
920 Commercial St.
Conyers, GA 30207
(misc. supplies)